# A SUPERGUIDE TO
# CATS

## HOWARD LOXTON

GALLERY BOOKS
An Imprint of W. H. Smith Publishers Inc.
112 Madison Avenue
New York City 10016

ISBN 0-8317 1200 7

Printed in Hong Kong

# CONTENTS

# INTRODUCTION

**European
Wild Cat**

A familiar cat sleeping, curled up in the living room, is a symbol of the home, of security and of peaceful domesticity. However, when the cat awakes, stretches its limbs, opens its eyes, yawns and shows its teeth, it changes into a symbol of the wild. Its tabby stripes become the marking of the tiger. Its eyes flash with predatory fire. Its paws unsheath their sharp and slashing claws and its teeth are the ravening fangs of the carnivore. Both images are true. The cat can be the most gentle and home-loving of pets, but it is also the cousin of the lion and tiger.

There are 36 species of modern cats in all. They include the Lion, Cheetah, Puma, Lynx, Bobcat, Jaguar, Ocelot, Serval, Caracal, Jaguarondi and Margay, as well as various smaller cats which are native in different parts of the world. Several of the small cats may have played a part in the development of the domestic cat. However, experts generally agree that the domestic cat's closest relations are the African Wild Cat (*Felis libyca*) and the European Wild Cat (*Felis silvestris*). The domestic cat can breed with them and feral animals may revert to the coat pattern and type of the wild cats after a few generations.

**African
Wild Cat**

The domestication of the cat is so recent, comparatively, that it has had only a superficial effect on the animal's physique and nature. Cats have learned to make the most of the homes and facilities that their owners provide. They show affection and sometimes, it seems, a genuine concern for people close to them. However, the physique and instincts of the domestic pet are still those of the wild cat. Its senses and skills are those of the predator. This fact is evident to anyone who has watched a cat about its daily business.

## THE CAT'S SENSES

Cats locate their prey by sight and sound and so both their eyes and ears are particularly sensitive. Compared with humans, cats only have a limited perception of colour and their eyes do not focus on very close objects. However, the popular belief that cats can 'see in the dark' has some measure of truth as the cat's iris can close to a narrow slit or open to a full circle. This controls the amount of light which enters the eye, enabling cats to register light such that they can see under circumstances which seem pitch black to us.

Cats can hear a far wider range of sounds than we can. A cat can not only hear but also locate the movement, because its ears are shaped and ridged to concentrate the sound. The ears are also highly manoeuvrable so that they can focus on a particular sound source and place its location. Cats can identify sounds with precision.

The cat may use its sensitive front paws to investigate an object, and quite a large area of the cat's

*Smell is one of the most important of a cat's senses. Long before a kitten's eyes are open, smell guides it to its mother's nipples.*

*Smell is used to mark territory and objects. When a cat rubs against a person's hand, glands on its head leave a scent behind.*

brain is devoted to handling messages from them. The nose is also very sensitive to touch and areas that will respond to even the slightest pressure are situated all over the body  Most important perhaps are the whiskers, eyebrows and long hairs on the back of the front paws. These are known as *vibrissae* and are all sensitive to pressure, even minute variations in the air around them which is affected by the presence of nearby objects. The cat can therefore judge spaces.

*Smell is used to identify objects or their past presence. A cat will 'nose' out food and prey and investigate new objects, especially shopping which may contain its dinner.*

The cat's sense of smell is also highly developed and is a major means of identifying both things and living creatures. It is the sense used by the newborn kitten before its eyes are open to find its way to its mother's nipples. It is also an important way of communicating territorial and sexual information. A cat will recognize friends and strangers by their smell and will reject or even attack the unfamiliar which seems to threaten danger.

A cat marks its claim to territory with its personal scent. It does this by spraying its urine against various places or by rubbing against them. In this way it deposits an identifying secretion from scent glands which are found by the anus, along the tail, around the lips and chin, and on either side of the forehead. Likewise, when a female cat is ready to mate, she produces a different scent which conveys this information to any male in the neighbourhood.

## FELINE COMMUNICATION

Aside from scent and visual signals cats communicate with each other by 'body language'. This is particularly noticeable when two cats confront each other. By making its fur stand on end and positioning itself to look as large and formidable as possible, a cat makes a show of strength towards another cat. The other cat, if it is prepared to give way without a contest, makes itself as small as possible, crouching low, dropping its head and being entirely submissive. Often an exchange of threatening displays, much hissing and growling, will end with one cat giving way.

*The whiskers, eyebrows and long hairs on the backs of the front paws aid the cat's spatial awareness by registering changes of pressure.*

*Cats are patient hunters and will wait in ambush or carefully stalk their prey.*

*By making its fur stand on end, a cat seeks to appear more formidable. When it rolls on its back, its belly is vulnerable but, in this position, it can lash out with its powerful back legs.*

*A cat can leap to considerable heights and across wide spaces. It judges distances with great accuracy.*

*Cats usually kill their prey by severing the spinal cord at the back of the neck with their teeth. If kittens are not exposed to live prey, they may never learn this killing bite.*

## THE HUNTER

The cat's keen senses and efficient body are designed to serve it in finding and obtaining food. The cat eats meat and, because it is a hunter rather than a scavenger, its eyes and ears are tuned to locating prey, while its limbs, sharp teeth and powerful claws are adapted to catching and killing it.

The cat is patient. It will wait for hours along a route where it knows that suitable prey will pass, waiting for the precise moment to pounce and kill. It stalks with stealth, keeping to cover or running almost flattened to the ground in exposed places. It will freeze, quite motionless, to avoid betraying its position. Caution and care increase as it approaches its prey, and ears and tail are kept low. After a trembling quiver passes through the hindquarters, there is a final dash and the victim will be struck down. Sometimes the cat lands close to its victim, keeping its hind feet on the ground to give stability against resistance and lunging forward to grip its prey on the back of the neck with a fatal bite. That is the way a cat usually catches rodents and other small animals which often form its prey, although sometimes it leaps down on them from above.

To catch birds, the cat must suppress its instinct to pause and pounce, which is something that not all cats can do, because birds can fly away between the cat's dash forwards and the final spring. Cats will leap to snatch a bird in its jaws as it flies away or strike it with a paw to knock it to the ground. Although cats have a reputation for catching birds, only a few are skilled at it. Cats catch insects in their jaws or swat them down and eat them while they are still stunned. Some cats even learn to fish. They dip a paw into the water and flip a fish on to the bank where they can grasp it firmly.

*Some cats can fish. They dip a paw into the water and, when a fish swims above it, they flip it upwards, out of the water and on to the bank where it can be gripped with the claws.*

6

## TRAINING AND LEARNING

Much of the cat's hunting behaviour is instinctive, but it seems that the method of killing prey by biting it in the neck has to be taught. Mother cats sometimes bring back live prey to their kittens as a means of teaching them. All the techniques of hunting and fighting can be seen in the play of kittens as they ambush, chase and fight each other. However, some built-in behaviour pattern prevents them taking their games too far so that no serious injury will be inflicted. Often a game will suddenly stop and kittens will change roles. A kitten pretending to be the prey changes places and becomes the hunter. The games which adult pet cats play are also closely related to hunting. Chasing, pouncing, catching and retrieving may be applied to a ball, a piece of string or a crumpled piece of paper, but these activities employ the same skills as those used by the wild cat in catching its prey and defending itself.

Except for Siamese, which are frequently precocious, kittens do not open their eyes till they are about nine days old and they cannot stand or walk well enough to wander far from the nest until they are about three weeks old. About a week later, they start to eat some solid food and the weaning process begins.

When the kittens are small, their mother will massage their anuses and genital areas to encourage them to excrete and wash them clean. When they begin to leave the nest, they will probably copy their mother in using a litter tray. However, it may be a little longer before they will copy her if she performs her toilet out of doors. They will also learn to wash themselves and each other. The cat uses its tongue and paws as a sort of scrubbing brush and face cloth. Its tongue can reach most of its coat directly, but it cleans its face and the top of its head by wetting its paws with its tongue and rubbing vigorously with them.

Kittens should not leave their mother for a new home until they are at least eight weeks old. By then they should be pretty independent, fully weaned and house-trained. Nevertheless, a new kitten may feel lonely without its mother, brothers and sisters. Once the excitement of being somewhere new gives way to the realization that it is on its own, the kitten will require a lot of comfort and reassurance. Talk to it quietly and make it feel welcome in your home, ensuring that other pets do not become jealous of or aggressive towards it. However, a kitten must not be spoiled. Start calling it by name and use a name which is easily said and easily recognizable. Decide on the rules you expect it to live by and be a gentle disciplinarian from the start. It is no use expecting a cat to understand that a misdemeanour you found amusing one day is forbidden the next.

*A cat's tongue can reach all parts except its head and neck.*

*In playing together, kittens develop and practise the skills which they will need to catch prey and to defend themselves.*

## CAT BREEDS

There are now well over 100 breeds and colour varieties of cats recognized by the Governing Council of the Cat Fancy in Britain. If one adds those new breeds seeking recognition and all the breeds and colours accepted in North America, which the British do not have, there is now an extremely wide range of cats. The rest of this book is devoted to a description of the recognized breeds and colour varieties, divided into three broad groups: the short-tailed cats which are described on pages 8–19; the long-haired cats on pages 20–31; and the so-called foreign short-hairs on pages 32–39.

# BRITISH SHORT-HAIR

All the wild members of the cat family have short coats and short hair. This also appears to be the normal type for domestic cats, because the genes for short hair are dominant over those for long. In Europe the standard pedigree short-haired cat is the British (and European) Short-hair.

The British Short-hair is a sturdy, well-built cat with a rather stocky look. Its compact, strong-boned skeleton is well-upholstered without being fat, and powerfully muscled. The shortish tail is thick at the base, tapering only slightly to a rounded tip. The legs are short and strong, with rounded paws. Set on a short, thick neck, the characteristically round head features full cheeks, a short broad nose, a firm chin, and large, round, widely-set eyes. The ears are small with rounded tips and a good covering of fur. The cat's coat is short and dense with fine, plushy-textured fur. The breed is recognized in a number of colour varieties, though not in all the cat colour types.

## BRITISH BLUE

The British Blue is a variety that often exemplifies the British Short-hair type. The coat is often more plush than in other colour varieties and the broad head and short nose often meet the standard more closely than other short-haired cats.

Blue, when used to describe the colour of a cat, is not a bright sky blue but a bluish-grey. Genetically, the colour is actually a dilute form of black. Many years ago, this variety used to be a dark slate blue colour, but a medium to light shade is now required by the standard. It must be an even colour all over, and must not shade from dark to light on different parts of the body. There must be no trace of stripes, bars or other patterning, nor should any white hairs occur in the coat. This cat's large, full eyes should be a rich copper or orange colour. Nose leather and paw pads should match the coat in colour.

The British Blue has a reputation for being a particularly placid and gentle cat. It is usually extremely intelligent.

## CHARTREUX

The Chartreux is a French breed. In Britain it is considered synonymous with the British Blue, but some American associations recognize it as a separate variety. The American cat has a broad head with full cheeks, but it is not so round and the ears are perhaps slightly larger and higher set than in the British Blue. The French strain was once more massive than the British and the French standard allows green eyes and a coat of any shade of blue.

## BLACK SHORT-HAIR

The coat of a Black Short-hair must be completely black without a single white hair, and each hair must be jet black to the roots. Kittens often have a brownish tinge to their fur and show faint tabby markings, but these usually disappear as the kittens grow older. Sometimes, the most un-promising kittens grow up with perfect coats. However, any trace of this 'rustiness' in an adult cat would be a fault. Cats often like to bask in the sun, but too much sun-bathing can produce this rusty tinge and so spoil a pedigree cat's show chances.

The Black Short-hair's physique should conform to the description given above for all British Short-hairs. Its eyes should be deep orange or copper in colour. The nose leather and paw pads should be black.

People once thought that black cats were associated with witchcraft and they were even believed to be one of the forms assumed by the Devil. Hence, in some European countries and in North America, they were often considered to be unlucky. In Britain, however, they are regarded as symbols of good luck. This is perhaps one reason why black cats are so popular. Although black cats may be common, one that fits the official standard is less frequently encountered. Often their bodies are too sleek. They may also have green instead of orange eyes, large, pointed ears, or a coat that is not pure black.

British Blue

Black Short-hair

## WHITE SHORT-HAIR

White cats should have coats that are pure white, without any coloured hairs or hint of cream. The nose leather and paw pads are pink. The eyes may either be a deep sapphire blue or a rich gold, orange or copper. In the variety known as 'Odd-eyed' one eye is blue and the other is copper. Because all kittens, whatever their breed, are born with blue eyes, it is impossible to determine the adult eye colour at birth.

White Short-hairs are not albino cats: they are genetically white. When also blue-eyed as adults, they are often deaf. This is not the result of any illness, but it is a disability that is genetically linked with the combination of a white coat and blue eyes. Kittens which have other colours in their ancestry often have a patch of darker fur. This frequently takes the

Orange-eyed
White Short-hair

Odd-eyed
White Short-hair

Cream Short-hair

because their coats make them more noticeable, and so they are more vulnerable to predators and more obvious to their own prey. Deafness in the Blue-eyed individuals would also make survival more difficult.

White coats show grease and other stains more than other colours and need more careful grooming. A dusting with talcum powder often helps to absorb grease and dirt. It can then be thoroughly brushed out.

In countries where the black cat was once thought to be unlucky, the white variety was the cat of good omen, but, in Britain, it was linked with bad luck. This superstition now seems to be forgotten, because white cats appear to be popular everywhere nowadays.

form of a smudge of colour on the top of the head between the ears. This will probably disappear as they grow older. However, this blemish is welcome, because it is a reassuring sign that the kitten's hearing is not affected. Orange-eyed Whites do not have this bias towards deafness, but it is sometimes claimed that Odd-eyed cats may have good hearing on one side while being deaf on the other. White cats also show a greater tendency than other colours to have extra toes. This condition is called *polydactylism.*

White cats are rare in wild or feral populations. Perhaps this is

## CREAM SHORT-HAIR

The Cream variety of British Short-hairs should have a light, even-coloured coat that is pale cream, not fawn or orangeish. Cream is genetically a dilute form of red and so when a Cream's colour is too 'hot', it is an indication of the red or tortoise-shell cats from which that Cream was probably derived.

Breeders have had difficulties in producing a variety that showed no trace of darker marking or of any white patches. Indeed, no red variety is recognized in the British Short-hairs because, in the full red, the tabby patterning persists so strongly. Cream kittens with dark markings frequently lose them as they reach maturity, but a spell of extreme weather—hot or cold—can sometimes make them reappear.

This variety must conform to the basic British Short-hair physical type. The eyes should be rich copper- or orange-coloured and the nose leather and paw pads should be red. Old books say that hazel-coloured eyes are permitted, but they have not been allowed in Cream Short-hairs since 1967.

## TABBY SHORT-HAIRS

Tabby markings must be the most familiar of all the cat coat patterns. It is the pattern of the wild cat of Europe and it is so dominant that it still shows in the kittens of other varieties that are solid-coloured when adult, and often in the grown cats themselves. The word *tabby* is said to come from the name Attibiya, a district of Baghdad, where a kind of taffeta or watered silk was made. This material gives a good idea of the pattern known as the classic, standard or blotched tabby.

There is also a striped pattern, suggesting the tiger, but this is now officially known as the mackerel pattern. The blotched pattern is thought to have developed from this. Two other patterns are closely linked to the basic tabby: the spotted and agouti-like coat of the Abyssinian. Both are mutations from it. Because both of these patterns are largely confined to separately recognized varieties, they are treated elsewhere (see pages 11 and 32). 'Lined' tabbies with narrow stripes some-times appear. They are thought to be a half-way stage between the mackerel and the agouti.

The classic tabby pattern is believed to have developed in Europe, where it was already becoming common by the mid-18th century. It spread from Europe, reaching India, for instance, about 100 years later. In Europe, the pattern is now very stable and more frequently encountered than the mackerel pattern. But in eastern countries, it is still variable. Its frequency fluctuates regionally. For instance, the vast majority of tabbies in London are blotched, but this does not hold for the whole of Britain. In Australia classic tabbies still seem to predominate.

Ancient Egyptian tomb paintings and Roman mosaics show mackerel tabbies. They also appear in European paintings by such artists as Pieter Bruegel (1525-1569). But John Aubrey, the English antiquarian, writing in the late 17th century, stated that tabby cats fetched high prices during the reign of Charles I because of their rarity. He called them Cyprus cats. Presumably people then thought that they came from Cyprus.

Today the exact patterning of both the classic and mackerel type is laid down extremely carefully. The classic tabby has three dark stripes running down the back and centred on the spine. Across the shoulders is a pattern shaped like a butterfly with front and hind pairs of wings, with spots within them. On each flank is an oyster-shaped blotch encircled by one or more unbroken rings. The tail is evenly ringed along its length and on the neck and chest are unbroken lines looking like necklaces—the more the better. The legs are evenly barred with bracelets that go all the way from the body markings to the toes. On the face, there are fine pencil markings on the cheeks and an unbroken line running back from the corner of the eye, an M-shaped mark on the forehead and a dark line running over the top of the head. The belly should be spotted.

The mackerel tabby has the same markings on the head, legs and tail as those of the classic tabby. On the body, there is only a single line running unbroken down the back from the head along the spine to the base of the tail. From this line, narrow lines run at right angles down both sides of the cat.

In both types, the markings are in a darker colour than the body of the coat and are clearly defined. The patches or lines should be continuous and not interrupted or broken up into spots, except on the belly. There must be no white patches, and each of the two colours should be even in shade.

The British Short-hair Tabbies are recognized in three different colour varieties: Silver, Red and Brown.

### Silver Tabby

The Silver Tabby has silver fur as the ground colour, with dense black markings in either pattern. The soles of the feet, from toe to heel, are black. The eyes are green or hazel and the paw pads are black. Nose leather should be preferably brick red, but a black nose is permissible.

Brown Tabby

Silver Tabby

Red Tabby

**Red Tabby**

The Red Tabby has a coat with a red ground colour and deep rich red markings in either pattern. The lips and chin are red and the sides of the feet dark red. The eyes are a brilliant copper. The nose leather is brick red and the paw pads are deep red.

**Brown Tabby**

The Brown Tabby has a coat of brilliant, coppery-brown fur, with markings of either pattern in dense black. The backs of the legs from paw to heel are black. The eyes may be orange, hazel or deep yellow in colour. The nose leather is brick red and the paw pads either black or brown.

**SPOTTED SHORT-HAIR**

The Spotted Short-hair was once known as the Spotted Tabby. Its links with the tabby are clear, because it has a strongly contrasting pattern similar to the mackerel tabby, except that the stripes are broken down into spots. A number of spotted cats

known in silver with black spots and green or hazel eyes; brown with black spots and orange, hazel or deep yellow eyes; and red with dark red spots and brilliant copper eyes. The nose leather and paw pads should be of the same colour as in the tabby.

Spotted cats often appear in the native populations of the eastern Mediterranean, but they are usually long-bodied, narrow-headed cats, with long, thin tails of the 'foreign' type. The Spotted Short-hair must conform to the physique requirements of the British Short-hair, as outlined on page 8.

**BI-COLOURED SHORT-HAIR**

The coat of the Bi-coloured Short-hair is clearly patterned in white and a darker colour. The second colour may be any one of those accepted for cats of all one colour: black, red, blue or even cream. The patches of colour should be evenly distributed, with not more than two-thirds of the coat coloured, nor more than one-half white. The patching should be carried

across the face, where a white blaze running from the cat's forehead to the nose is desirable. There should be no sign of ticking or barring on the coloured fur and no stray coloured hairs within the white areas. A symmetrically balanced pattern is preferred. The eyes should be brilliant copper or orange.

**BLUE-CREAM SHORT-HAIR**

This two-colour variety is not a patched cat. Instead of the clearly defined pattern of the Bi-coloured Short-hair, it has a coat in which the blue and cream fur are softly intermingled. There must *not* be a blaze on the face and, nowhere, especially on the paws, should there be a clear area of fur of unbroken colour. There should be an even balance of blue and cream over the whole coat. Naturally, there should be no tabby markings or patches of white. Eyes are copper or orange, the nose leather blue, and the paw pads blue or pink or a mixture of both. Like all British Short-hairs, this variety has a compact body and a round head with full cheeks.

Spotted Short-hair

were apparently around at the end of the 19th century and some even had face markings broken into spots. In the 20th century, however, they were hardly known until the variety reappeared in a British show in 1965.

The ideal Spotted Short-hair would have well-balanced, rounded spots. But triangular, star-shaped and rosette-like markings are all currently acceptable in the coat. The pattern must not consist of narrow or elongated markings which simply look like the broken stripes of a mackerel tabby. The tail should have spotting or broken rings, the legs should be spotted and the face should have typical tabby markings.

The Spotted Short-hair may be any colour of those recognized for cats with fur of all one colour, with appropriate colour spotting and eyes to match. However, it is mainly

Bi-coloured Short-hairs

Blue-cream Short-hair

## TORTOISESHELL SHORT-HAIR

Tortoiseshell cats have a three-coloured coat consisting of black clearly patched with cream and red on all parts of the body, face, legs, feet and tail. The three colours should be proportionally well-balanced. A cream or red blaze on the face is considered desirable. The eyes are brilliant copper or orange, the nose leather and paw pads being either pink or black or having patches of both colours.

Tortoiseshell cats are nearly always female. When males are born, they are almost all infertile, although two tortoiseshell males were recorded as siring kittens about 80 years ago. To produce tortoiseshells, breeders must mate a tortoiseshell mother with a tom cat that is of good British Short-hair type in one of the accepted colours that make up the tortoiseshell coat. Breeders avoid tabbies, because they are likely to pass on their patterning, which is difficult to eradicate in future generations. The kittens produced may include self-colour blacks and reds as well as tortoiseshells. The tortoiseshell kittens are often very dark-coated when they are born. As they become older, however, the colours become brighter. Adults with the best markings usually develop from such individuals. Tortoiseshell kittens sometimes occur when an all-black cat and an all-red cat are mated.

## TORTOISESHELL AND WHITE SHORT-HAIR

This variety has the three-coloured markings of the Tortoiseshell, combined with a partly white coat. The cheeks, top of the head, ears, back, tail and part of the flanks are covered with a clear, balanced patching of black, red and cream. This colouring should also appear on the paws. The underpart of the body, chest, legs and chin are white and a white blaze on the face is desirable, but tortoiseshell areas must always predominate over the white. The eyes are copper or orange. The nose leather and paw pads are pink or black or they are patched with both colours.

Like the Tortoiseshell, the Tortoiseshell and White Short-hair is basically a female-only variety and the females must be mated to males of other patterns. Although breeding records indicate some unusual sires, including a Blue Long-hair, the obvious choices would be male Bi-coloured or self-coloured of a good type.

## SMOKE SHORT-HAIR

The coat of the Smoke Short-hair may be either black or blue, with an undercoat of pale silver. When still, these cats look as though they have a solid coat of a dark colour. But the

Tipped Short-hair

silvery undercoat shines through when they move. The eyes are yellow or orange and the nose leather and paw pads are black or blue to match the colour of the coat.

## TIPPED SHORT-HAIR

The British Tipped Short-hair has a white undercoat and topcoat. But each hair on the back, flanks, head, ears and tail is tipped with colour. The tipping is evenly distributed to give a sparkling effect. It may also slightly shade the legs, but the chin, stomach, chest and undertail should be as white as possible. The Tipped Short-hair is recognized in all the colours of short-hair, uniformly coloured cats, and also in brown, chocolate and lilac. In all colours, the nose leather and paw pads should be either pink or correspond to the colour of the tipping as closely as possible. Cats with black tipping have green eyes. Others have rich orange or copper-coloured eyes.

This breed was originally created by mating Short-hair Silver Tabbies to Long-hair Chinchillas. The resulting colour variety was a short-haired equivalent to the Chinchilla (see page 24).

Tortoiseshell Short-hair

Tortoiseshell and White Short-hair

Smoke Short-hair

# AMERICAN SHORT-HAIR

Variously known as the American Short-hair, the Domestic Short-hair and the American Domestic Short-hair, this breed is very similar to the European short-haired cats with which it shares its origins. It was, in fact, developed from cats taken to North America by immigrants from Europe, but there are now distinct differences between the two types.

The American Short-hair is less cobby than the British Short-hair and has a somewhat longer look. Its head is less round than the British variety, being more heart-shaped. Its ears are less open at the base, while its eyes have a hint of a slant at the outer edge. The short, thick fur has a much harder texture than the European Short-hair. American varieties are recognized in a wider range of coat colours and patterns, although not all the organizations in North America recognize all the varieties.

Blue American Short-hair

### RED AMERICAN SHORT-HAIR
A red self-coloured cat is recognized in this breed. In the British type, tabby markings have proved too predominant for it to become an accepted colour. The coat is a deep, rich, brilliant red, with no shading, marking or ticking. The lips and chin are the same colour as the rest of the coat. The nose leather and paw pads are brick red and the eyes are a brilliant gold.

### CHINCHILLA AMERICAN SHORT-HAIR
The Chinchilla is the American equivalent of the black variety of the British Tipped Short-hair (page 12).
In Britain this is only one of the possible colours of a breed that did not gain recognition until 1978. The American cat was recognized much earlier.

### WHITE AMERICAN SHORT-HAIR
This variety has a glistening, pure white coat, with pink nose leather and paw pads. It may be blue-, orange- or odd-eyed, like the British White Short-hair (see page 9).

### BLACK AMERICAN SHORT-HAIR
This coal black cat with golden eyes is similar to the British Black, except in the ways described above and in that the paw pads may be brown or black.

### BLUE AMERICAN SHORT-HAIR
Pale coats are preferred in this colour, but a level tone is more important and a darker cat of an even shade will be preferred to a light-coloured cat of uneven colour. (See also the British Blue, page 8).

Red American Short-hair

It has a pure white undercoat and the topcoat is tipped with black on the back, flanks, head and tail, giving a sparkling silver appearance. The chin, stomach and chest must remain pure white, although the legs may be slightly shaded. The rims of the eyes, the lips and the nose are outlined in black, but the nose leather is brick red. The paw pads are black and the eyes a rich emerald or blue-green. (See also Chinchilla Long-hair, page 24).

### SHADED SILVER AMERICAN SHORT-HAIR
This cat is a darker version of the Chinchilla in which the tipping on the spine is dark, becoming lighter as it shades to the white underparts.

### CAMEO AMERICAN SHORT-HAIR
Shell, Shaded and Smoke Cameos are all recognized in the American Short-hair. The first two are red versions of the Chinchilla and the Shaded Silver, respectively. The Smoke Cameo, which is also known as the Red Smoke, is an even darker red. They all have rose-coloured nose leather and pads and brilliant gold eyes. (See Cameo Long-hairs, page 25).

### SMOKE AMERICAN SHORT-HAIR
The Black Smoke is like the British cat, apart from following the American physical type. Its white undercoat is covered by a jet black coat that gives the cat a solid black appearance except when it is in motion. Nose leather and paw pads are black and the eyes are a brilliant gold. The Blue Smoke has a blue topcoat and blue nose leather and paw pads.

### TABBY AMERICAN SHORT-HAIRS
In addition to the Silver, Brown and Red Tabby varieties, which are recognized in the British Short-hair (see pages 10–11), the American Short-hair may also be Blue Tabby, Cream Tabby or Cameo Tabby. The patterns in all cases are like those described for the British Tabby Short-hairs (page 10) but, naturally, they must all conform to the American Short-hair physical type.

The Blue Tabby has a ground colour of pale, bluish-ivory, with contrasting markings in a deep blue. It has brilliant gold eyes, rose paw pads, and 'old rose' nose leather.

The Cream Tabby has a pale cream ground colour to the coat, with darker markings in buff or cream. These markings provide a good

Chinchilla American Short-hair

Shaded Silver American Short-hair

Shell Cameo American Short-hair

Smoke Cameo American Short-hair

Shaded Cameo American Short-hair

contrast, but they remain within a dilute colour range without becoming reddish. It has brilliant gold eyes and pink nose leather and paw pads.

The Cameo Tabby has an off-white ground colour, with red markings, rose nose leather and paw pads, and brilliant gold eyes.

### TORTOISESHELL AMERICAN SHORT-HAIR
This is a tri-coloured cat like the British Tortoiseshell Short-hair in colour and pattern (page 12), but it follows the American Short-hair standards in other respects.

### PARTI-COLOUR OR BI-COLOUR AMERICAN SHORT-HAIR
This cat is like the British Bi-colour, with patches of solid colour on white. The patches may be black, blue, red or cream. The eye colour in all types is a brilliant gold.

### TORTOISESHELL AND WHITE AMERICAN SHORT-HAIR
This cat is similar in pattern to the British Tortoiseshell and White Short-hair, but the exact requirements regarding the extent of the white areas of the coat of this variety differ

from one American association to another. In some associations, this variety is replaced by the Calico (see below), while some associations recognize both. The eyes are gold.

## CALICO AMERICAN SHORT-HAIR
In some American associations, this cat is the equivalent in pattern and colour to the British Tortoiseshell. In others, it is a similar cat, but it has a white coat with tri-colour patches, rather than one divided into coloured and white sections. It can also be a cat with a white ground, patched only with black and red (no cream). The eyes are gold.

## DILUTE CALICO AMERICAN SHORT-HAIR
The dilute form of the Calico is a white cat, patched with unbrindled (clear-coloured) areas of blue and cream. The eyes are brilliant gold.

Cameo Tabby
American Short-hair

Cream Tabby
American Short-hair

Blue Tabby
American Short-hair

Calico American
Short-hair

Dilute Calico
American Short-hair

## BLUE-CREAM AMERICAN SHORT-HAIR
The coat on the body, face and extremities of this variety is broken into clearly defined patches of the two colours—the exact opposite of what the British standard requires. The eyes are brilliant gold.

Blue-cream
American Short-hair

Exotic Short-hair

## EXOTIC SHORT-HAIR

This variety was created in the United States by crossing American Short-hairs with Persian (Long-hair) cats. This crossing produced a type that had the physique and hair texture of the Persian, but with short fur. It is probably the closest of the American breeds to the British Short-hair, although it is not quite the same. There is a similarity in that, to re-establish the type in the British cat after the interruption to pedigree breeding during World War II, British breeders also introduced long-hair blood to the British type.

The Exotic has a cobby body, set low on short legs, with a deep chest and equally massive shoulders and rump. The middle section is short and well-rounded. The round and massive head has a broad skull and is set on a short, thick neck. The short tail is usually carried without a curve and at a lower angle than the back. The small, low-set ears are wide apart, tilted forward and round-tipped. The chin is full, as are the cheeks. The nose is short and broad, without a break, and the eyes are large and round. The paws are large and round, with close-set toes. The coat is soft and dense and longer than in the American Short-hair.

It may be solid colour white (odd-eyed, blue-eyed or orange-eyed), black, blue, red or cream; of either mackerel or standard tabby in silver, red, brown, blue, cream or cameo; chinchilla, shaded silver, shell or shaded cameo; black, blue or cameo smoke; tortoiseshell, calico, dilute calico, blue-cream or bi-colour. The requirements for coat pattern, eye colour, nose leather and paw pads are the same as for American Short-hairs of the same colour.

## AMERICAN WIRE-HAIR

This variety appeared as a natural mutation in a litter of farm cats in New York State. The kitten had a coat like that of a Wire-hair Terrier dog, but it was even coarser and with hair tightly curled on the head and ears. The original cat and its immediate descendants tended to have rather longer legs, heavier hips and shorter heads than the American Short-hair. Breeders now aim for a cat like the American Short-hair in all respects except for the texture of the coat, which should be of medium length and very wiry on the head, back, sides, hips and along the top of the tail. It can be less coarse on the underside of the body and on the chin.

American Wire-hair

# UNUSUAL SHORT-HAIRED CATS

## MANX

True Manx cats have no tail, not even the vestige of one. At the end of the spine, where the vertebrae should start to form the tail, they are completely missing and it is possible to feel a hollow at the end of the backbone. This gives the cat a very rounded rump—'round as an orange' is how the British standard used to describe it. The back legs are longer than the short front legs and the hind quarters are carried high, giving an upward slope to the line of the back, although this is often somewhat off-set by the bending of the rear legs. In motion the cat seems to have a bobbing, or rather rabbit-like, gait.

In Britain the head should be as near that of the British Short-hair as possible and the nose should be straight. In North America, a definite dip in the nose is preferred by some breeders. The cheeks are prominent. The ears are larger than in the British Short-hair, pointed and set higher on the head. The coat is double, with a thick undercoat and a longer outer-coat. Colour and markings follow those permitted for British and American Short-hairs.

All sorts of legends explain how the Manx came to lose its tail. One tells how it was late arriving at the Ark and slipped in just as Noah was shutting the door, trapping its tail and leaving it behind. Another legend relates that it was bitten off by a cat to save her kittens from soldiers who used to kill cats to use their tails as helmet plumes. But taillessness is, of course, a genetic aberration that has been perpetuated. Tailless cats have appeared in various parts of the world, but the name Manx, which refers to the Isle of Man, is significant because an island home is a restricted breeding area. This helped to ensure the recurrence of the type despite the fact that the genetic coding that causes a kitten to be born without a tail is often linked with physical and health problems. Sometimes the re-duction of vertebrae is not restricted to the tail and a malfunction of the sphincter muscles is also associated with the malformation. There is a tendency to a high mortality rate and true Manx bred to true Manx through several generations may bear dead kittens. Breeders must be careful to avoid perpetuating such problems.

Manx

Rumpy (tailless)

Longy (longer tail)

Stumpy (short tail)

Even when both Manx parents are completely tailless, some kittens in the litter will probably have tails, either complete or reduced in length. 'Stumpy' (short-tailed) and Tailed Manx are now recognized as British varieties. Some American organiz-ations recognize five different stages from the tailless to the completely tailed. The stages are called Rumpy (tailless), Riser (with a small number of vertebrae which can be felt or seen), Stubby (with a distinct and moveable short tail), Longy (with a longer but not a full-length tail), and Tailed.

Manx may be any colour or pattern, with eyes matching the coat as described for other colour varieties.

## SCOTTISH FOLD

The Scottish Fold is a variety of cat with dropped ears. It developed from a chance mutation which appeared in Perthshire, Scotland, in 1961. Its development has caused much controversy among cat lovers. It is not accepted as a breed in Britain, although a Fold kitten won a prize in a British show in 1971. However, the judges considered the kitten to be a normal prick-eared cat, because its ears had not, at that stage, developed the characteristic droop. In North America, the type has gained favour with some breeders and has been accepted as a registered variety by some organizations.

Because the original mutant was bred to British Short-hairs, the cat is of basic British Short-hair type. It is cobby-bodied and round-headed, with a short neck. Its coat is short and soft. The ears are usually small and they fold forward and down at the top of the ear pocket, making it difficult to clean them properly. The fold may be only slight in kittens, but there must be a definite fold line in adults.

In North America, the Scottish Fold is accepted in the following colours: white, black, blue, red, cream and cameo; chinchilla, shaded silver, shaded and shell cameo; black, blue and cameo smoke; tortoiseshell, calico, dilute calico, blue-cream and bi-colour. The eyes and leather should be the same as for short-haired cats of the same coat colour and pattern.

Scottish Fold

## REX

Rex cats are another comparatively recent development. They result from a natural mutation which affects the cat's coat and which also occurs occasionally in other animals, including rabbits.

The fur of most cats is made up of several kinds of hair. There are long, straight, thick hairs which taper evenly; curving hairs which thicken and then taper suddenly; crimped hairs which are somewhere between the other two; and down hairs which are evenly thin and crimped.

In most cats, there are 50 times as many of the last type of hairs as there are of the first. But, in the Rex cat's coat, the fur consists almost entirely of down hairs or, in one type, of down hairs plus a small proportion of the third type of crimped hair. The length of individual hairs is only about half that of the fur of normal short-haired cats and its thickness is reduced by more than a third. The result is a short, plushy coat with a rippling waved effect, which is especially noticeable on the back. The whiskers and eyebrows are crinkly.

The first cat known to have this kind of coat was born in Germany in the 1940s. In the 1950s this cat produced kittens in East Berlin. Imported into the United States, these kittens played a part in the development of the North American Rex variety. There were also two isolated mutations in the United States: one

Cornish Rex

Devon Rex

in Ohio in 1953 and another in Oregon in 1959. But, by then, breeding had already begun from Rex cats imported from Britain.

The British Rex strains have their origins in a cat with Rex-type fur born to a Cornish farm cat in 1950 and a cat born in neighbouring Devon ten years later. In Britain, they are recognized as two separate varieties.

## BOMBAY

This American variety was created by breeding a Black American Short-hair to a Burmese. This produced a cat with the colour and type of the Short-hair and the sleek coat of the Burmese. The head is round with a full face and considerable breadth between the eyes, tapering, with a definite nose break, to a short, well-developed muzzle. The large, round eyes are yellow to deep copper in colour, the darker the better. The body is neither cobby nor rangy and the tail is straight and of medium length. The short, close-lying coat has a fine, satin-like texture and a sheen like patent leather, a feature particular to this variety.

Bombay

## SPHYNX

The Sphynx is a variety, not recognized in Britain nor by several of the American cat associations, which has been developed from a chance mutation which appeared in a litter born in Ontario, Canada, in 1966. The mother was a black and white domestic pet and her kittens were quite normal except for one which had no hair!

Hairless cats have appeared before in other places. Among them were a pair of Siamese born in France and another pair in London. In fact, none were completely hairless, except at birth.

The Sphynx has a covering of soft, downy hair. This hair is hardly perceptible except on the large ears, the muzzle, tail, feet and the testicles of the males, where it is tightly packed and more noticeable. There may also be a ridge of short, wiry hair down the spine and the face is covered with a soft pile. Eyebrows and whiskers are lacking. The cat's coat feels like suede to the touch.

Although not developed from oriental-looking cats, the Sphynx, like the Rex and the only two similar British cats the author has seen, has the long body, long, tapering tail, neat, oval feet and more wedge-shaped head of the foreign type. The mutation of the fur appears to be connected with an overall change in physique.

Sphynx breeders say that these cats prefer people to other cats. But they do not like being cuddled, although

Sphynx

they will settle on a friendly lap, sometimes standing with one front paw lifted, a typical stance for this variety.

Sphynx have a high body temperature. They sweat and, without a coat to retain their heat, they like a warm environment. When it is cold, they will snuggle up against a heat source even more than other cats, but they are not frail cats and should be strong and muscular.

The skin of adults should be taut and wrinkle-free, except for the head, although kittens often look as though they have a skin several times too large for them, because it is loose and puckered. The rather barrel-shaped chest of the Sphynx encourages a slightly bow-legged look, which is particularly noticeable in kittens. Except for its sloping eyes, the cat looks from the front a little like a Boston Terrier dog. The Sphynx coat may be in any of the colours accepted for short-haired cats.

# LONG-HAIR (PERSIAN)

It is generally thought that the earliest long-haired cats were probably like modern Angora cats and came from Turkey. However, by the mid-19th century a heavier type, known as the Persian, was more popular. The modern long-hair type recognized in Britain and the American Persian are the same variety and were developed from it.

The Long-hair has a short, cobby body, short thick legs and large, round feet. The head is round and broad, with full cheeks and a short nose. The coat is luxuriant and flowing. There is a full ruff around the neck and over the top of the chest, a sumptuous tail and long tufts on the ears and between the toes. Long-hairs are recognized in a wide range of colour varieties and the equivalent Persian in even more colours.

## BLACK LONG-HAIR (BLACK PERSIAN)

The Black Long-hair should have an absolutely pure black coat, but perfect specimens are not common. Even a single white hair will show clearly against the raven black coat. A slight rustiness may also show up in the fur in certain lights, especially when the cat is moulting or if it has been basking in sunshine for long periods. Owners are advised, after brushing and grooming, to rub the fur with a piece of silk or chamois leather in the direction of the lie of the coat. This final touch will give the cat an extra, glossy sheen. It will also help to remove any stray white hairs which tend to be of a coarser texture than the rest of the fur. Black Long-hairs should have the shape and build of their type. The jet black fur should be matched with black nose leather and paw pads, and the large eyes should be copper or deep orange.

Black Long-hair

## WHITE LONG-HAIR (WHITE PERSIAN)

Like its short-haired counterpart, this variety may have either blue eyes, orange eyes, or one eye orange and one blue, the colours being rich and brilliant. Originally, only the blue-eyed type was known. However, this White had perhaps more Angoran ancestry than other Persians and Blue Long-hair blood was introduced to improve the long-hair appearance of the cat. This crossing brought in the orange eye colour and odd eyes. Because of this background of crossings, a mating between cats of the same eye colour often produces a litter including kittens with any of the three types. The linking of the white coat and blue eyes carries an hereditary tendency to deafness. However, a kitten which has any dark patch of fur is not usually deaf, even though the patch will disappear as the cat matures.

The White Long-hair should have a pure white coat, without any mark or blemish. Its nose leather and paw pads should be pink.

White Long-hair

## BLUE LONG-HAIR (BLUE PERSIAN)

The British standard for this variety allows the coat to be any shade of blue, provided that it is even in colour and free from any marking or white hairs. Lighter shades are definitely preferred in North America, although evenness of colour is more important than its strength. The Blue Long-hair's eyes are deep, brilliant copper or orange. Nose leather and paw pads are blue. This variety has a particularly full ruff around the neck and over the chest.

## RED LONG-HAIR (RED PERSIAN)

Long-hairs with all red fur are recognized on both sides of the Atlantic. Solid red, or red self, cats have been developed from Red Tabbies. The tabby markings which persist so strongly in short-haired red cats are not so noticeable in long-haired cats, although it is rare to find them completely lacking, especially from the face. Kittens which are strongly marked at birth may take 18 months to two years to get their final coat, so there is plenty of time for the pattern to fade. In the past this variety has been known as an orange or a marmalade cat, but the colour should be truly red, although at the orange end of the red range.

The lips and chin should be the same colour as the coat, not white or cream as is often the case. The whiskers should also be red. The eye colour is deep, brilliant copper. The nose leather and paw pads are brick red. Red coloration is caused by a gene which appears to be sex-linked, and, because red females are comparatively rare, crossings with Black and Tortoiseshell cats have been used to produce solid Reds.

Blue Long-hair

Red Long-hair

Cream Long-hair

## CREAM LONG-HAIR (CREAM PERSIAN)

The cream coat colour is created by the combination of the genetic coding for both red and for a dilution of colour. This variety owes its development possibly to both the offspring of very pale Reds and to matings between Red and Blue Long-hairs. Some early cats of this variety were fawn in colour, but a paler shade is now expected. Because the red element is sex-linked, cream females are produced only when cream is mated to cream, or in pairings where both parents carry both red and dilution factors. Eyes in the Cream Long-hair must be a rich copper colour. The nose leather and paw pads are pink.

Silver Tabby Long-hair

### Brown Tabby Long-hair (Brown Tabby Persian)

The British standard for this variety describes a pattern with the butterfly wings outlined across the shoulders and deep bands running down the saddle and sides. There is no mention of the usual whorls of the classic pattern, nor of the mackerel type. However, the two usual patterns are both recognized as separate varieties and, in practice, are accepted in Britain. The coat should be a rich tawny brown, with clear black markings. There is often a tendency to lighter, or even white patches on the chin and around the lips, but this

Brown Tabby Long-hair

Blue Tabby Persian

Red Tabby Long-hair

### TABBY LONG-HAIR (TABBY PERSIAN)

Tabby long-haired cats may have either the classic or the mackerel type tabby markings (see page 10).

In either case the markings must be clearly defined, although long fur tends to make their edges softer than in short-haired cats, and the strength of contrast between ground and pattern varies from colour to colour.

Cream Tabby Persian

### Silver Tabby Long-hair (Silver Tabby Persian)

This is a truly beautiful cat, although Silver Tabbies may not always satisfy those who like an extreme Persian-type head. This is because the nose and face tend to be less flattened than in some other varieties. The pattern of lustrous black on a silver ground, matched to bright green or hazel eyes with red nose leather, will always win admirers. The paw pads are black.

Cameo Tabby Persian

Many of the most attractive Silver Tabbies are extremely dark at birth, almost solid black except on the legs and sides. The markings begin to separate from the coat as the kitten grows and may not be complete until it is about six months old.

is a definite fault. The eyes are copper or hazel in colour. The nose leather is red and the paw pads are either black or brown.

### Red Tabby Long-hair (Red Tabby Persian)

The Red Tabby's coat should be a rich red, with markings boldly defined in an even darker red. The eyes are deep copper in colour. The nose leather is brick red and the paw pads are pink.

### Cream Tabby Persian

The British Cat Fancy does not yet recognize a Cream Tabby Long-hair, but it is accepted in North America. The ground colour, including the lips and chin, is a pale cream. The markings are in buff or a cream sufficiently darker than the body of the coat to give a good contrast. The eyes are bright copper or gold and the nose leather and paw pads are pink.

### Blue Tabby Persian

The Blue Tabby is another variety recognized in North America but not in Britain. The ground colour is a pale, bluish-ivory, including lips and chin, with deep blue markings. The whole is permeated with a warm fawn overtone. The eyes are brilliant copper or gold. The nose leather is old rose and the paw pads are rose. This colouring has occurred spontaneously in litters of brown tabbies. It can also be produced by mating Brown Tabbies to solid Blues.

### Cameo Tabby Persian

The Cameo Tabby is another colouring recognized in North America, but not in Britain. The Cameo Tabby has an off-white ground colour, with red markings. The eyes are bright copper or gold. The nose leather and paw pads are rose.

### PEKE-FACED PERSIAN

This is a variety which has been known in North America for nearly 50 years, but the British Cat Fancy has not approved it. The Peke-faced Persian's coat may be either red-tabby or solid-red.

The variety follows the usual Persian type, looking very like other Persian cats except for its face. This has a pushed-in frontal look, with a retroussé (upturned) nose, and heavy wrinkles on the muzzle and from the corners of the eye. The eyes are large and round and somewhat protrusive. As the name of the variety suggests, it closely resembles a Pekinese dog. While these cats can have considerable charm and personality, they are similar to Pekinese, Pugs and other dogs with flattened faces, in that they risk developing breathing problems because of their extremely short noses. The fold of skin beneath the eyes can sometimes cause the tear ducts to become blocked. Another danger is that the teeth of the upper jaw do not meet correctly with those of the lower jaw.

Breeders must be extremely careful not to perpetuate any deformity that is harmful to the animal. This problem is inherent in aiming for such an extreme appearance, so unlike the original feline type. Some kittens display the characteristic break between the nose and the forehead within a day or so of their birth. Others do not develop it for up to six months.

Peke-faced Persian

## CHINCHILLA LONG-HAIR
## (CHINCHILLA PERSIAN)

The Chinchilla's pure white under-coat, topped by a long, silky fur which is tipped with black on the back, flanks, tail, head and ears, makes it an especially striking cat. It is also known in the United States as the Silver Persian.

In Britain it is accepted that this is usually a smaller and more dainty looking cat than the other varieties of the long-hairs. In North America, however, it is expected to be of full Persian type. The emerald or blue-green eyes, which are heavily out-lined by dark rims of black skin on the edges of the eyelids, and the brick red of the nose leather enhance the effect. The paw pads are black.

It is said that the Chinchilla was created in Britain in the 1880s when a breeder crossed a Silver Tabby Long-hair with a Smoke Long-hair and the earlier version of the breed was much darker than the modern cat. Chinchilla kittens are nearly always born with quite dark fur and noticeable tabby markings, especially on the tail, which disappear as they grow older.

Shaded Silver
Persian

Chinchilla
Long-hair

Blue-smoke
Long-hair

Smoke
Long-hair

## SHADED SILVER PERSIAN

If one thinks of the Chinchilla as the Silver Persian, then the Shaded Silver Persian might aptly be called the Pewter Persian. It is exactly like a Chinchilla except that the tipping of its fur is heavier, giving it a much darker overall look. The shading should grade evenly from dark on the spine to white on the chin, chest and stomach, with the legs matching the face in tone.

Both Chinchillas and Shaded Silvers can be born in the same litter and it is not possible to tell the variety of the youngest kittens, because the darkest ones sometimes mature to have the lightest coats. In Britain it was found to be extremely difficult to decide the variety of even an adult cat. In 1902, therefore, it was decided to drop the Shaded Silver category, but it is still considered a separate variety in North America and Australia. Like the Chinchilla, the eyes are deep green or blue-green, the nose leather is brick red and the paw pads are black.

## SMOKE LONG-HAIR (SMOKE PERSIAN)

The Smoke Long-hair may have derived from crossings between Blacks and Whites and other long-haired cats. It has a white undercoat, while the uppercoat is heavily tipped with black. The tipping is darkest on the back, head and feet and shades to silver on the sides. When the cat is still, the general effect is of a black cat. When it moves, the white undercoat shows through clearly. The fur on the feet and the face is black except at the very base of each hair, where there is a narrow band of white. The generous ruff and ear tufts look silver. The eyes are brilliant copper or orange. The nose leather and the paw pads are black.

## BLUE SMOKE LONG-HAIR (BLUE SMOKE PERSIAN)

The Blue Smoke is identical to the Black Long-hair in all save the colour of the coat, which is deeply tipped with blue, and the nose leather and paw pads which should also be blue. The eyes are copper or orange.

## SHELL CAMEO PERSIAN

This variety is a red version of the Chinchilla, produced by crossing Chinchillas and solid Reds. They have been recognized for 20 years in the United States. However, they still await breed status in Britain, although they have been seen for many years. The American standard describes the undercoat as ivory

Shaded Cameo Persian

Smoke Cameo Persian

Shell Cameo Persian

white. British breeders aim at a colour from off-white to a light cream. The uppercoat is very lightly tipped with red, making this a cat with no more than a pink blush to its coat. British breeders will also accept cream tipping, but this is not permitted in North America. The top of the head, ears, back and the upperside of the tail should all be lightly tipped, shading to a totally untipped chin, chest, stomach and underside to the tail. The ear tufts are untipped, but the face and legs may be lightly tipped. The large, copper-coloured eyes are outlined by rose-coloured rims to the upper and lower eyelids. The nose leather and paw pads are also rose.

## SHADED CAMEO PERSIAN

This cat is a slightly darker form of the Shell Cameo, to which it is identical in all respects other than the depth of the colour.

## SMOKE CAMEO PERSIAN

Also known as the Red Smoke, this cat, the darkest version of the Cameo, is indeed the red equivalent of the other Smoke varieties. Various bodies specify slightly different shades for the undercoat from white or ivory to cream. The uppercoat is so heavily tipped with red that the cat appears to be solid red in repose. The pale undercoat is revealed only when it moves. This variety is like the other smokes in all respects except colour, with red substituted for blue or black in the coat, and the nose leather, eye rims and paw pads being of a rose colour.

Bi-colour Long-hairs

colour. Both Blue and Cream are dilute forms (of black and red). Most Blue-Creams are female and no record exists of successful mating from a Blue-Cream male. Blue-Creams are occasionally born to Tortoiseshell mothers and such cats are, in effect, dilute forms of tortoiseshell. More frequently, however, Blue-Creams are born to Blue and Cream crosses. In such crosses, breeders avoid the risk that red colouring from the Tortoiseshell will persist.

## TORTOISESHELL LONG-HAIR (TORTOISESHELL PERSIAN)

The three colours which make up the tortoiseshell coat, red, cream and black, should be evenly distributed and well-broken into patches on the body, face, legs and feet. A cream or red blaze from the nose to forehead is considered an enhancement. Black must never be the dominant colour in the coat. It is more difficult to obtain clearly defined areas of the three colours in a long-hair and the hard-edged patches of short-haired cats should not be expected.

The eyes should be copper or deep orange. The nose leather and paw pads should be tri-coloured like the coat.

This is another variety in which like-to-like matings are not possible.

## BI-COLOUR LONG-HAIR (PARTI-COLOURED PERSIAN)

The British standard for this variety allows the coat to be any solid colour and white. In North America, however, where it is also known as the Parti-coloured Persian, it is restricted to white with either black, blue, red or cream. The patching of the long, silky coat should be clearly defined and the patches of colour should extend over the face. A white blaze between the nose and forehead, or as an inverted V over the face, is particularly liked. The large, round eyes should be deep orange or brilliant copper in colour. The nose leather and paw pads should be in accordance with the coat colours.

## BLUE-CREAM LONG-HAIR (BLUE-CREAM PERSIAN)

In North America the Blue-Cream variety is like a Parti-coloured cat. Its coat is patched distinctly with the two colours. In Britain, on the other hand, the colours should merge and intermingle to give an effect somewhat like shot silk. American breeders like to see a cream blaze running down from the forehead. Eyes should be deep copper or dark orange in

American Blue-cream Long-hair

British Blue-cream Long-hair

A Black or Cream male is often used, or a solid-red if one with an un-marked coat is available. Red Tabbies should be avoided, because the offspring would probably carry the tabby pattern. Litters will contain a mixture of colours. Depending on the colour of the stud cat, the kittens may be cream, black, blue-cream or red. There is no guarantee that a litter will include a single tortoiseshell.

## TORTOISESHELL AND WHITE LONG-HAIR (TORTOISESHELL AND WHITE PERSIAN)

In Britain the wording of the standard for Tortoiseshell and White Long-hairs describes a coat that is slightly different from that of the Tortoiseshell and White Short-hair. It states that the three-colour patching shall be broken and interspersed with white, rather than requiring the colours to be mainly on the back and upperpart of the cat and the white below. However, there must still be a good balance between the colours and white, which must not be too dominant.

Some American standards specify a pattern more like the short-hair with white legs, feet and underparts, extending halfway up the body, and with white splashes on the nose and half way around the neck. The eyes should be deep orange or brilliant copper. The nose leather and paw pads should have broken colour, like the coat. In some American associations, the Calico is the same as the British Tortoiseshell and White. Males are extremely rare.

## CALICO PERSIAN

This North American variety may be either a cat with a white ground coat patched with red and black, or a white cat patched with red, black and cream. Its belly should be white and there should be predominantly white areas on the chest, legs, paws and face, preferably including a white blaze. The variety sometimes forms the American equivalent of the Tortoiseshell and White Long-hair. In other associations, it exists as a distinct variety alongside it. The Calico will usually carry more white in the coat than the Tortoiseshell and White. Male Calico cats are extremely rare and usually sterile.

## DILUTE CALICO PERSIAN

This cat is similar to the Calico, except that its patching is of blue and cream on white (blue and cream being the dilute forms of black and red). White should predominate on the underparts. The eyes are brilliant copper.

Tortoiseshell Long-hair

Tortoiseshell and White Long-hair

Calico Persian

Dilute Calico Persian

# OTHER LONG-HAIRED CATS

## ANGORA

Angora cats got their name from the Turkish city of Angora, which we now call Ankara. Their silky fur is like that of the Angora goat (mohair), which comes from the same area, and the Angora rabbit was so named because of its similar coat. Although Angoras were probably the first long-hairs in Europe, interest passed to the heavier Persian cat in the last quarter of the 19th century and, in Turkey itself, the Angora almost disappeared. It was saved from extinction by a specially organized breeding programme at Ankara Zoo.

In 1963 permission was given for a pair of Angora cats to be taken from Ankara to the United States. Three years later, another pair were also exported. The breed was re-established in the United States from these four cats. Angoras are now being bred in Britain but they are not sufficiently widespread there for them to be recognized as a breed.

The Angora has a longish body and tail and a small, neat head, with large, upright ears. The eyes are large and almond-shaped, with a slight slope upwards. The legs are long, with small, round, dainty paws. The back legs are longer than the front legs, so that the rump is carried slightly higher than the rest of the back. The tail is long and tapering. When the cat is on the move, the tail is often carried forward horizontally over the back. The medium-length coat tends to waviness, especially on the stomach. There are tufts of hair between the toes and at the ear tips. There is also a good furnishing of hair in the ears.

The Angoras bred at Ankara Zoo are all white cats and this is now the accepted colour for the variety. Eyes may be blue, amber or one of each colour. White, blue-eyed cats may be deaf, as in other varieties (see page 20). The paw pads, lips and nose leather should be pink. In the past, the Angora was known in black, blue and other colours, and may be so again. This affectionate cat is said to be adept at learning tricks.

Angora

## MAINE COON CAT

This personable American variety of cat got its name partly from the eastern seaboard state of Maine and partly from a belief that it derived from a cross between a raccoon and a domestic cat. Such a mating could not possibly produce kittens and can be ruled out.

Maine Coon Cats certainly lack the cobby, short-bodied, low-slung look of the Persian and their fur is not so long. Although they are often large cats, some weighing as much as 13.5 kg (30 lb), they have quite delicate-looking faces, with high cheek bones, large upright, pointed ears, slightly slanting, oval eyes and a long nose, with little or no break. The neck, body and tail are all long, and these strong and sturdy cats have powerful muscles and substantial legs.

Surviving in the countryside through rigorous Maine winters, this cat has developed a rugged coat. Its fur is not as long as the Persian's, but it is quite heavy. It is relatively short on the shoulders, becoming gradually longer towards the tail and ending in shaggy, heavy breeches around the flanks. It gets gradually longer at the sides towards the stomach. The fur on the tail is long and full. There is a frontal ruff beginning at the base of the ears and the ears themselves are well tufted.

The Maine Coon Cat can have a wide range of coat colours and patterns: white, black, blue, cream, all colours and types of tabby, tortoiseshell, tortoiseshell and white, calico, blue-cream and bi-colour. It may also be tabby and white, a coat not recognized in either American or British Short-hairs or in Persian cats. The eye colour may be shades of green, gold or copper. The colours do not have to agree with the coat colour as laid down for other varieties. White-coated cats may also have blue eyes or odd-coloured eyes. The nose leather and paw pads should match the coat.

Maine Coon Cat

## COLOURPOINT (HIMALAYAN)

The Colourpoint Cat is of the Persian type, but it has the coat pattern and colours of the Siamese. In North America, it is called Himalayan. The term Colorpoint is used to describe another variety

This cat has a low, cobby body on short but sturdy legs, small, low-set ears, a short nose and full cheeks, and round eyes as close as possible to the Long-hair (Persian) type. The eyes are always brilliant blue. The coat is long, thick and soft in texture and there is a full frill over the neck and chest. The tail is luxuriant. There are long tufts at the ears.

Colour and pattern follow those of the Siamese, with face mask, ears, legs and feet and tail of a darker coloured fur, set off against a pale body colour. In addition to the original seal and blue, there are now a number of other colours. Those recognized in Britain are chocolate, lilac, red, tortie (tortoiseshell) and cream, all of which are Siamese colours, and a blue-cream, chocolate-cream and lilac-cream, which are not accepted in the Siamese. In North America, there are even more colours, because the Tortie may be seal, cream, blue or lilac, each combined with red and/or cream. They may also be red, lilac, chocolate or seal lynxpoint (like the Lynx or Tabby-point Siamese).

Colourpoints
(Himalayans)

## CYMRIC (LONG-HAIRED MANX)

This American cat is in all respects like the Manx (see page 17), except for the length of its fur. It was not created by crossing Manx with long-haired cats. Instead, it developed from a long-haired kitten, a mutant born in a litter of other short-haired Manx cats. Its parents and ancestors were pedigree Manx going back through several generations.

The Cymric (meaning Welsh), the name by which it is known in Canada, or Manx Long-hair, as it is known in the United States, has a medium length coat, which is softer than that of the normal Manx. The variety has the final vertebrae missing, the longer back legs and the same overall physical balance of the short-haired version. It is recognized in the same coat and eye colours.

Cymric (Long-haired Manx)

## BIRMAN

The Birman is another long-haired cat with a pattern of darker points like that of a Siamese, although the Birman has white paws. It is not of the Persian type and it does not have the usual long-hair type in its ancestry. It is said to be a variety first known in Burma and to have links with Tibet and Kampuchea.

In North America the 'golden' colouring is seen today as a pale fawn to cream in the Seal variety of the Birman, although it is claimed that cats with pure blood-lines from the original strain have a golden halo to the whole back of the coat. A golden look is certainly expected in Europe. The British standard describes the coat as beige that is slightly golden. It has coloured points and mask like the Siamese, but the paws look as though the cat has walked into a saucer of milk. The white 'gloves', as they are called, extend to an even line across the paw at the third joint and up the back of the hind legs to end in a point. The white areas on the back of the legs are known as the 'laces'.

The Birman has a long but fairly stocky body. The head is broad and rounded, unlike either the Siamese or the Persian, because it has a nose of medium length. The ears are larger than the Persian's and both the tail and legs are longer. The fur is long and silky in texture and tends to curl on the stomach. There is a ruff around the neck. The medium-length tail

Blue Point Birman

Seal Point Birman

has a plume of long, silky fur, unlike the bouffant Persian.

The original variety of Birman, as the legend of its colouring describes, was the Seal variety with a beige coat, seal-brown points and nose leather, pink paw pads (again unlike the Siamese), white 'gloves' and bright blue eyes. The Blue Point

came next. It has a bluish white body colour, shading almost to white on the stomach and chest and with deep blue points. The nose leather is slate grey, the paw pads are pink and the eyes are blue. Chocolate and Lilac Point Birmans are also recognized in North America. Their colouring follows that described for the Siamese.

Ruddy Somali

Red Somali

## SOMALI

This variety is a long-haired version of the Abyssinian Cat (see page 32). It has not yet achieved recognition in Britain. It first appeared as a natural long-haired mutation probably in Canada, but also in the United States and Europe.

It has exactly the same physique as the Abyssinian. The body is long and lithe and the tail is thick-based and tapering. The head is a slightly rounded wedge, with large, pointed ears and almond-shaped eyes. The coat has the same agouti-ticked fur and the same facial markings, but it is long, soft and silky, with horizontal tufts in the ears and tufts at their tips. The tail is plume-like and a generous ruff and breeches are desirable. The coat may be either ruddy or red in colour. as in the Abyssinian. The eyes are a rich gold or a deep green in colour.

Ragdolls

## RAGDOLL

This North American breed looks like the Birman in physique and coat. As originally bred and first accepted by one American association, its colour and markings resembled those of the Birman. Some other associations now also recognize both a bi-colour and a colourpoint version (that is, patterned like the Siamese with dark paws). However, it is not its appearance that makes the Ragdoll so different from any other cat.

The first Ragdolls were a litter of kittens born to a cat that had been injured in an accident. The kittens were all extremely relaxed, even limp, like a ragdoll hanging over the arm—hence the name. They appeared to feel no pain and to have little sense of fear or awareness of danger. Such characteristics are unlikely to help them to protect themselves or to avoid injury. They are placid and calm cats, with extremely quiet voices.

The original type of Ragdoll had the 'white gloves' of the Birman. This is the only variety recognized by the original breeder and one American association. Others have developed and gained acceptance from other associations for both the bi-coloured and colourpoint varieties (see page 29), and in them the original form is called the 'mitted'. Ragdolls tend to be large cats, with thick fur which forms a fluffy ruff and a long, full tail.

## BALINESE

This is another naturally occurring, long-haired mutation from a short-haired cat, in this case from the Siamese. It has the full Siamese-type head, body, tail and legs, the same vivid blue, oriental eyes, and the contrasting coat pattern of dark mask and points set against a lighter ground colour. It also has the lively personality and intelligence of the Siamese cat.

American breeders were the first to recognize their attractiveness. By breeding the naturally occurring long-haired mutants to each other, they produced a cat with luxuriantly long fur. There is now enthusiastic support for the Balinese in Britain, although there are not yet enough cats in the country for the variety to gain recognition. In North America, the Balinese is accepted in Seal Point, Blue Point, Chocolate Point and Lilac Point. It is possible that a wide range of colours will eventually gain recognition in Britain. Unlike other long-hairs the Balinese' coat does not form a ruff.

Seal Point
Balinese

## TURKISH CAT

The body of the Turkish Cat is long and sturdy, with medium-length legs and rounded feet. The head is wedge-shaped, but not so long as in the Siamese, although the nose is long. The ears are large, upright and set fairly close together. The eyes are round and light amber in colour. The fur is soft, long and silky. It has no woolly undercoat. The tail is full, the ears well-feathered, and there are tufts of fur between the toes. The coat is chalk white overall, with the exception of the medium-length, well-furnished tail, which is auburn, with faint, darker rings. There are also auburn markings on the face which extend from the base of the ears, but leave a white blaze between them, the ears themselves being white. The nose leather and paw pads are pink, as are the insides of the ears, and there are rims of pink skin around the eyes. Turkish cats of other colours can be seen in Sweden. These came from other provinces of Turkey.

Males, in particular, are sturdy and muscular, especially on the neck and shoulders. They are hardy cats. In their native countryside, they must endure snow for half the year. They have earned the nickname of 'Swimming Cats'. Turkish Cats really seem to enjoy being in water. They even like to be bathed, as well as swimming in shallow streams.

# FOREIGN SHORT-HAIRS

Cats in this groups are also sometimes known as 'orientals' and, originally, some of them did come from the East. However, the word 'Foreign' in the name refers only to their type and not to their countries of origin. The most familiar and typical of cats of this group are the Siamese and their derivatives.

In general Foreign Short-hairs have wedge-shaped heads, with large, pricked ears and slanting eyes, slim bodies on long legs, and a long, tapering tail. However, there are numerous small differences from breed to breed.

Foreign Short-hairs are not usually solitary creatures. They like company, feline or human. If their owners are away from home all day, they are happier if there is another animal to share their lives. They tend to mature earlier than cats of the other groups and females often begin to 'call' when only six months old.

Blue Abyssinian

Sorrel (Red) Abyssinian

## ABYSSINIAN

The Abyssinian cat was first listed as a separate breed under that name in 1882. Its origin is a matter of conjecture. It has been claimed that it is a direct descendant of the cats of the Egyptian pharaohs and that it was brought to Britain from Ethiopia by soldiers returning from the Zulu wars in 1868. It has also been suggested that it is the result of a careful breeding programme by British breeders who wanted to produce a cat like the ancient type and who used tabbies which appeared with the agouti pattern of individually striped hairs which sometimes occurs in tabby lines. However it came about, the Abyssinian's coat does have similiarities with that of the African Wild Cat and its form closely resembles some of the cats depicted in ancient Egyptian paintings and sculptures.

This medium-sized cat has a firm and muscular build, but it is elegant and lithe. The body and the tapering tail are fairly long. The legs are slim, with small, oval feet. The head is broad and wedge-shaped, but gently contoured without flat planes. The muzzle is not pointed and is shaped by a shallow indentation on either side. There is a slight rise from the bridge of the nose to the forehead, a gentle rounding to the brow and a firm chin. The ears are large, broad-based, gently pointed and preferably tufted. The eyes are large and almond-shaped.

The Abyssinian coat is made up of short, fine fur, of which each hair is striped with two or three bands of colour. There should be no barring or stripes on the legs, chest or tail, though there should be a solid area of darker colour at the tail tip and up the back of the hind legs. There is a line of darker colour around the eyes and dark lines also extend from the corner of the eyes over the forehead. These and the eye outlines are set against lighter fur. Many Abyssinians have white patches around the lips and over the lower jaw. These are undesirable. If they extend on to the neck and undercarriage, they constitute a definite fault.

Two colours of Abyssinian are recognized in Britain and North America. A third, the Blue, is provisionally recognized in Britain.

## RUSSIAN BLUE

Russian Blues were at one time known as Archangel Blues. It is thought that sailors brought these cats back to Britain from the port of Archangel, in northern Russia.

The Archangel cat had a small, triangular head set upon a long, slender body. Its coat was thick, soft and silky. For hundreds of years, cats with blue coats were known as Maltese cats and sometimes as Spanish cats.

The modern form of the breed has a short, wedge-shaped head, with a straight nose, strong chin and prominent whisker pads. The almond-shaped eyes are vivid green and set well apart. The ears are large and pointed, wide at the base and set vertically on the head. The skin is thin and transparent, with little inside hair. The body is long and graceful, with long legs and small, oval feet and a fairly long, tapering tail. The double coat is soft, silky and very thick. It is an even and clear blue throughout, with a distinct silvery sheen. The nose leather and paw pads are blue.

The British cat is still of a rather more foreign type than is preferred in North America, where the ears are not so pointed and are set lower on the head. Lighter shades are preferred in the coat and American descriptions specify silver-tipping of the guard hairs, slate grey nose leather, and paw pads of lavender pink or mauve.

Russian Blue

## EGYPTIAN MAU (ORIENTAL SPOTTED TABBY)

This variety was produced in a conscious attempt to create a cat which would look like those in ancient Egyptian paintings and sculptures. Whereas the Abyssinian suggests the type and is similar to the African Wild Cat, the Egyptian Mau, as it was first generally known, is like those spotted cats seen in murals and on papyri.

The North American Mau line has a geographical link with Egypt because the cats are derived from animals which came from Cairo via Rome. Three were shown at a cat show in Rome in the mid-1950s. They were the first of the breed in North America, establishing two colour varieties: the Silver and the Bronze.

In Britain the Mau did not have its origin in imported cats but in tabby kittens of foreign type which appeared during the breeding of the Tabby Point Siamese. Acknowledging its ancestry, its British name was changed to the Oriental Spotted Tabby when it received official recognition as a breed in 1978.

The British cat is of extreme foreign type, being in effect a spotted Siamese. It has striped limbs, a ringed tail and tabby markings on the head, which include a pattern on the forehead like that of a scarab beetle. This beetle features in Egyptian art and religion and often appears on the foreheads of cat figures. The eyes are green. The coat can be of any of the accepted tabby colours.

The American cat is of less foreign type. Although the eyes are oval and slightly slanting, fully oriental eyes are considered a fault. The body is slightly more cobby than in the Siamese and the head is a more rounded wedge. Several colours are now recognized by various associations.

Egyptian Maus
(Oriental Spotted Tabbies)

# SIAMESE

The Siamese does have a genuine connection with Siam, or Thailand as it is now called. Thailand, however, is not necessarily the country where the breed originated. The characteristic pattern of the coat has appeared occasionally as a mutation in many lands and it seems likely that the Siamese probably developed first even farther east.

The modern Siamese cat is extremely elegant and svelte. It is of medium size, with a long body, slim legs and dainty, oval feet, the hind legs being slightly longer than the front ones. The tail is long and thin and tapers to a point. The head is wedge-shaped, with a smooth outline both in profile and from the front. There may be a slight change in angle at the top of the nose, but otherwise it narrows in perfectly straight lines from large, wide-based, pointed ears to a fine muzzle, with a strong chin and a level bite. There should be no pinching in of the cheeks nor any roundness. The eyes are almond-shaped and placed at a slight angle to the nose. They should be a clear, deep blue, whatever the colour of the coat, except for those which are lilac-pointed or lilac-pointed tabby, when the British standard allows for eyes of lighter blue.

## SEAL POINT SIAMESE

The body colour of an adult Sea Point Siamese is cream, shading into a pale, warm fawn on the back It will be paler in kittens and, in mos cats, there will be some darkening of the back with age. The mask, ears, legs, feet and tail are clearly defined in seal brown. This rich, dark brown is genetically black, being lightened slightly by the same genetic coding that controls the pointed pattern. No dark marks should occur anywhere else, although a number of cats have a dark blotch on the belly. Light 'spectacles' around the eyes or light patches on the feet would disqualify a cat from exhibition in a show, but these features are now rare. The nose leather and paw pads should match the points in colour, except in North America, where the paw pads may be pink.

## CHOCOLATE POINT SIAMESE

The Chocolate Point, a further dilution of the Seal, was seen occasionally among the earliest Siamese. It was then often considered to be a poorly coloured Seal. However, it owes its colouring to a different gene. Chocolate Points were not officially recog-

Seal Point Siamese

nized until 1950, at first in Britain and then in other countries. The body colour is ivory, shading, if at all, to the colour of the points. The points are the colour of milk chocolate. The nose leather and paw pads match the points or, in North America, they are described as cinnamon pink and pink.

## BLUE POINT SIAMESE

The Blue Point was the second of the Siamese colours to be recognized. It was appearing regularly in both British and American shows by the

1920s. The first was registered as long ago as 1894, before the standard for the Siamese was firmly established.

The cat's body colour is a glacial-white shading into blue on the back, but even there it is of a lighter tone than the points and mask which should be a clear blue, the ears being of even colour with the mask and limbs. The eyes are a clear, vivid blue. The nose leather is slate blue, as are the paw pads in Britain, but the paw pads are pink in North America.

Blue Point Siamese

Lilac Point Siamese

## LILAC POINT SIAMESE (FROST POINT SIAMESE)

In the United States, the Lilac Point Siamese was originally known as the Frost Point. Its colouring occurs when both parents carry recessive genes for both Chocolate and Blue. Lilac Points bred to Lilac will produce lilac kittens.

The body colour is off-white. The standard for British cats describes the shade as magnolia. In North America some associations ask for milk white or glacial-white. The mask

and points are pinkish-grey according to the British standard, with nose leather and pads of faded lilac. In North America, the description is given as frost grey, with a pinkish tint, and the nose leather and pads are described as faded lilac. In North America the eyes should be deep or brilliant blue, but the British standard allows for a light, but not pale, vivid blue in this colour variety.

Chocolate Point Siamese

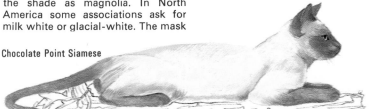

### RED POINT SIAMESE (RED COLORPOINT SHORT-HAIR)

The Red Point variety of the Siamese was first recognized in North America in 1956. Recognition came a decade later in Britain. This variety has a white coat, with shading to pale apricot being permitted on the back. The points are a bright reddish-gold according to the British standard, with the legs and feet being reddish-gold to apricot. In North America the colour is described as deep red. The nose leather and paw pads are pink. The eyes are vivid blue.

Some American organizations refuse to recognize any colours other than Seal, Blue, Chocolate and Lilac as true Siamese. They call them Colorpoint Short-hairs.

### TABBY POINT SIAMESE (LYNX POINT SIAMESE, OR TABBY COLORPOINT SHORT-HAIR)

As is obvious from its name, the Tabby Point Siamese has the points and mask of the Siamese in the form of tabby markings.

The body colour should be of the appropriate colour to match the colour of the points, as described for that particular colour Siamese. The legs have broken horizontal stripes of varying size, with the back of the hind legs of solid colour. The tail is marked with many clearly defined rings and ends in a solid-coloured tip. The mask has clearly defined stripes, especially around the eyes and nose and on the forehead, with distinct markings on the cheeks and darkly spotted whisker pads. The ears are solid-colour without stripes, but there is a pale smudge on the back of the ears, like the impression of a thumb. The nose leather and paw pads conform with the colours described for the Siamese of the colour

of the markings, or they may be pink. The eyes are brilliant blue, with the lids either darkly ringed or toning with the points.

### TORTIE POINT SIAMESE (TORTIE COLORPOINT SHORT-HAIR)

This is a female-only variety. It can be produced when a Seal Point is mated with a Red Point, or when a Tortie Point is mated with any other Siamese colour. The points are a bi-colour or tri-colour mixture of red and/or cream, with either seal, blue, chocolate or lilac. The body colour is the equivalent of whatever is appropriate to the incorporated colour. Feet, legs, tail, ears and mask should all be made up of mingled colours, as should the nose leather and paw pads. However, the distribution may be random and it does not have to follow a regular pattern.

American organizations, which do not recognize this colouring in the Siamese, class this variety as a Tortoiseshell Colorpoint Short-hair.

### CREAM POINT SIAMESE (CREAM COLORPOINT SHORT-HAIR)

The Cream Point Siamese, a further dilution of the Red Point, has a white body coat. If there is any shading, it is only of the palest cream. The points are a cool, clotted cream shade, warming towards apricot on the nose, ears and tail, but avoiding a hot shade. The nose leather and paw pads are pink. The eyes are a vivid blue. This is another variety which is grouped with the Colorpoint Short-hairs by those who do not class it as Siamese. Cream Point Siamese almost always carry tabby markings. They are then indistinguishable from Cream Tabby Points.

Tabby Point Siamese

Red Point Siamese

Tortie Point Siamese

Cream Point Siamese

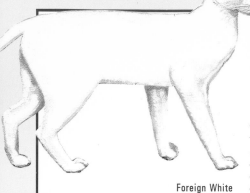

Foreign White

## FOREIGN WHITE

The Foreign White is another form of Siamese, although it lacks the distinctive Siamese point pattern in its coat, which is completely white. The paw pads and nose leather are pink and the eyes are brilliant blue.

In this variety, the genetic factor which restricts the coloured fur of the Siamese to the mask and points is so dominant that it removes them altogether. The cat is not an albino and there is none of the pinkness about the eyes that is common to albinos of all species. When the breed was being created from Siamese in which the colour restriction was extreme, there were problems in that the deafness associated with blue-eyed white cats appeared. However, by careful selection in breeding, experts believe that inherently deaf strains have been eliminated.

In North America this variety would be grouped with other cats of Siamese type that are of one colour. These cats are called the Oriental Short-hairs (see opposite).

## FOREIGN BLACK

The Foreign Black is another variety originating from the Seal Siamese. It is the opposite in development to the Foreign White, being a Siamese in which the restriction factor has become so recessive that it has ceased to be effective. Not only does the colour extend over the whole of the cat's coat, but the dilution effect, which creates the seal tone, has also been lost so that the cat has glossy black fur all over. The eyes are green. The paw pads and nose leather are black. The Foreign Black has the characteristics of the Siamese in every other way. This cat was recognized only recently in Britain. The corresponding breed in North America is the Ebony Oriental Short-hair.

## FOREIGN LILAC

Lilac cats are produced when both parents carry the genes for both blue and chocolate and some examples of a Siamese cat with a solid lilac coat appeared during the creation of the Havana. During the 1960s, breeders began to give attention to its development as a distinct type of Siamese, whose soft and glossy coat is frost grey with a pinkish tone. The nose leather and paw pads are pinkish. The eyes are vivid green. The corresponding breed in North America is the Lavender Oriental Short-hair. It is also sometimes known as the Foreign Lavender.

Foreign Lilac

Foreign Black

## HAVANA (HAVANA BROWN)

The Havana is a Chocolate Siamese in which the dilution factor does not operate, leaving the glossy coat a rich, chestnut brown throughout, being slightly darker than the colour of the ancestral Chocolate. The whiskers and nose leather are the same colour as the coat, but the paw pads are pinkish-brown. The eyes are green, but oriental in shape and setting. The head, ears, body, legs and tail all follow the standard for the Siamese in shape and balance, at least in British and European cats.

The first Havanas in North America came from Britain. However, the American strain, now called the Havana Brown, was not crossed back to Siamese and a different cat has resulted. It has a more rounded muzzle, round-tipped ears, a distinct stop level with the eyes, and a slight break behind the whiskers. Its eyes are dark green in colour and the nose leather is rosy in tone.

Havana

## ORIENTAL SHORT-HAIRS

This is the name under which all the solid coloured Siamese cats are grouped by North American associations. This group does not include the Havana, which is less Siamese in type than it is in Britain and Europe, but it does include the equivalents of the British Foreign White (opposite), the Foreign Black, known as the Ebony in North America (opposite) and the Foreign Lilac, known as Lavender (opposite). In addition the group includes many other colours that are not recognized in Britain: Blue, Chestnut, Red, Cream, Silver, Cameo, Ebony Smoke, Blue Smoke, Chestnut Smoke, Lavender Smoke and Cameo Smoke. Also recognized are both classic and mackerel tabby patterns of Ebony, Blue, Chestnut, Lavender, Red, Cream, Silver and Cameo and Tortoiseshell, Blue-Cream, Chestnut Tortie and Lavender Cream.

These cats have the physique of the Siamese, but their eye colour is green or amber, except for the White, which may have blue or green eyes. However, the White may not be odd-eyed. Oriental short-hairs tend to have softer voices than the Siamese.

Oriental Short-hairs

## JAPANESE BOBTAIL

The Japanese Bobtail is a variety that occurred naturally in Japan and owed nothing to artificial breeding. It has been known there for hundreds of years and is one of the types of cats which appears in Japanese paintings, sculptures and wood-block prints. The facade of the Gotokuji Temple in Tokyo is decorated with many pictures of these cats in a welcoming posture, with one paw raised. They are the *Maneki neko*, or the welcoming cats.

This cat does not fit into any of the basic physical types. Although more slender than the British or American Short-hairs, it does not have the full foreign look. The head is a triangle with gently curved sides. It has high cheek bones and a noticeable whisker break. The ears are large and upright, set more across the head than at the sides. The large eyes are oval and set at a slant. The Japanese Bobtail has long legs. The hind legs are longer than the front legs, but they are usually held bent when the cat is relaxed. This means that the body line remains level.

This breed's most distinctive feature is its tail, from which it gets its western name. At first sight the tail looks short and fluffy, like that of a rabbit. It often looks shorter than it is, because it is carried crookedly. There is a short straight section, only a few centimetres long, and there may be an angled section. The tail fur is longer and thicker than the rest of the coat, giving a pom-pom effect.

Japanese Bobtails

Japanese Bobtails can be produced in many colours. It is the *Mi-Ke*, the tortoiseshell pattern, however, which the Japanese associate with good luck. It is this cat which sets the pattern for the variety as accepted in North America. The coat is soft and silky and of medium length. It may be any of the combination of colours that make up the *Mi-Ke*: black, red and white; red and white; black and white; tortoiseshell or tortoiseshell and white; and solid coloured black, red or white.

# BURMESE

The Burmese cat seems genuinely to be a cat of the Orient and the female from which the western breed was developed was taken to North America from India. It is thought to have been a hybrid between a Siamese and a cat with a dark coat and, in North America, it was mated with a Siamese.

However, the Burmese is now a distinctly different type of cat from the Siamese. It has neither the extreme type of the Oriental, nor the cobbiness of the British Short-hair. Its body is of medium length, with a build that is more heavy and muscular than its appearance suggests. The chest is strong and rounded and the back is straight. The tail is of medium length, tapering only slightly to a rounded tip. The head is slightly rounded on the top, with full, wide cheeks, and tapers to a short, blunt wedge. The ears have slightly rounded tips and a forward tilt. There is a distinct nose break and a strong lower jaw. The eyes are large with the top edge having an oriental slant, while the lower edge is rounded. The coat is short, fine and close-lying,

## BROWN BURMESE (SABLE BURMESE)

In Britain the Brown Burmese is described as a warm seal brown. Kittens and young cats may be lighter and even show tabby markings. The nose leather is a rich brown and the paw pads are brown.

In North America the brown variety is known as the Sable Burmese. Some associations recognize only this original colour in the Burmese.

## CHOCOLATE BURMESE

The Chocolate Burmese is a British variety. The coat is a warm, milk chocolate colour, with chocolate brown nose leather and paw pads of brick pink, shading to chocolate.

## RED BURMESE

The adult in this British-recognized variety has a coat of light tangerine. The ears are distinctly darker than the back. Slight tabby markings are permissible on the face. The nose leather and paw pads are pink.

**Brown Burmese**

**Chocolate Burmese**

## LILAC BURMESE

Another British variety, the Lilac Burmese has a pale and delicate dove grey coat which has a slight pinkish tinge, giving a rather faded effect. The nose leather is lavender pink. The paw pads of kittens are shell pink, gradually becoming lavender pink with age.

**Red Burmese**

**Blue Burmese**

with a satiny texture. It is particularly glossy. An even less Siamese look is required in North America than in Britain, with more rounded eyes. The feet should also be round, not oval as in the British standard.

## BLUE BURMESE

The standard for the Blue Burmese in Britain asks for a soft, silver grey coat, with a distinct silver sheen on rounded areas, especially the ears, face and feet. The nose leather is very dark grey and the footpads are grey.

The American standard calls for a rich blue, with the same iridescent sheen. The nose leather and paw pads are blue-grey with a pinkish tinge.

**Lilac Burmese**

## BLUE-CREAM BURMESE

The Blue-Cream Burmese is another British-recognized colour variety. The coat is a mixture of blue and cream with no obvious barring. The colour and markings are less important than the Burmese type. The nose leather and paw pads are plain, or blotched blue and pink.

Blue-cream Burmese

Tortie Burmese

## CREAM BURMESE

The Cream Burmese, another British variety, has a rich cream coat when adult and may show slight tabby markings on the face. The ears are very slightly darker than the colour of the back. The nose leather and the paw pads are pink.

Cream Burmese

## TORTIE BURMESE

The Tortie Burmese, with the usual tortoiseshell mixture of brown, cream and red, is recognized in Britain. The colour and markings, however, are not so important as the overall type. The nose leather and paw pads may be plain, or blotched brown and pink.

## TONKINESE

This relatively recent American hybrid breed was created by crossing the Siamese and the Burmese, between which there are greater differences in North America than in Europe.

The Tonkinese is a medium-sized, well-muscled cat. The head is a slightly rounded wedge, with a squarish muzzle and a rise from the bridge of the nose to the forehead. The ears are of medium size, with rounded tips, and they are tilted slightly forward. The feet are oval and the tail is tapering. The rich blue-green eyes are almond-shaped and slightly oriental.

The Tonkinese is now recognized in several colours. In all of them, the mask and points of the Siamese still show through as darker fur, but they do not have clearly defined edges. Instead, they merge gently into the body colour. The Natural Mink has a coat of warm brown, with dark chocolate to sable points. The Honey Mink has a more reddish-brown coat, with reddish points. The Tonkinese has also been produced in rich chocolate brown, champagne and blue-grey coats.

Tonkinese

## KORAT

The Korat is a cat from Thailand, but it is very different from the cats we know as Siamese.

It is a medium-sized cat. It is sturdy and muscular, with a medium-length tail that is heavy at the base and tapers to a rounded tip. The back is carried in a curve. Its legs are shorter than those of the Siamese. The face is heart-shaped, with a large, flat forehead and a strong but not sharply pointed muzzle. In profile there is a slight stop between the forehead and the nose, which has a slightly downward curve. Its ears are large and upright, with rounded tips. Its eyes are large and spaced widely apart.

The coat is a silvery blue which is unlike that of any other breed. The silver tipping of the coat increases as the kitten matures, reaching its full strength at about two years old.

Korat

# INDEX